I would like to thank my friends
Klementyna de Sternberg
Stojalowska and Jim Jordan,
without their support this guide
would never have happened.

What's inside this book?

Introduction
Step up!

"It's a step up" they say in the advertisement promoting the introduction of the living wage. They are correct, but it comes at a cost. The expected increase to payroll is 18%. **Yes, 18%.**

With that in mind, you may want to revisit your selling prices and, of course, staff efficiency. Reducing number of employees or reducing staff cost, following the strategy B&Q and Zizzi's who cut staff benefits, may be the go-to approach for reducing overheads, but savings can be made in areas that may not be obvious. In the coming pages we will identify and explore areas of savings hidden across your business.

I'm not a petrol head, but there is one motoring strategy that I am a fan of: Mazda's Gram Strategy.

If you are looking for improving your performance, there are two options: expand resources or streamline the structure. This one focuses on the latter. In the world of motoring, Mazda became a hallmark of smart improvement. By applying this strategy to your business, you can become one too.

In 2014, a record breaking 581,173 businesses were registered with Companies House. It's great news as it means the economy's improving, but it also means it's harder to stand out. In addition, statistics tell us that half of the new businesses fail within 5 years.

So, what makes the other half thrive and grow irrespective of the economic climate, new taxes and other government surprises?

Mazda Gram Strategy

Third generation of Mazda MX 5 was to be bigger than its predecessor. The challenge for the manufacturer was to come up with a way of achieving this goal without compromising its characteristic of a lightweight roadster. They succeeded; the new model was larger yet only 10 kg heavier. It was possible thanks to their new 'gram strategy'.

During development, every component was scrupulously analysed with a view of finding ways of making it lighter, but without sabotaging safety or performance. This includes, for example, using aluminium instead of steel (wherever possible), making components smaller, and making shapes more efficient. Engineering teams had targets for creating lighter elements and whole modules. Each gram was important, every little change made an impact. This approach was to become a part of their new development process.

The fourth generation of Mazda MX-5 is an amazing 100kg lighter still.

They've created a superstar lightweight roadster. According to their website Mazda MX-5 is still the best selling two-seater sports car ever.

In the dawning age of the living wage, the first instinct is to cut overheads. This, unfortunately often means reducing staff or cutting down your shopping list. But think about it for a minute. Limited resources may mean limiting chances of getting through the crises, not to mention this may hinder your chances of growth and destroy your competitive edge. I know there is another way. A way of limiting expense without compromising your position on the market.

Inspired by Mazda's gram strategy I am investigating how successful businesses manage their expenses and how they are finding those pennies that add up to pounds. Adjusting an expense policy is a standard in the era of agile business and you have probably already made some changes to help you manage your spending more effectively.

However, we tend to focus on the big one-off rewards and overlook the smaller amounts that over time add up to significant numbers.

I analyse the spending patterns and discover how much we can salvage from the most unexpected expenditure areas in business.

This book will help you:

- Manage your expenses and identify which overheads can be cut to lighten the burden of your business

- Reduce overspending by planning plan ahead and avoiding costly traps of contracts you and your business may not need

- Streamline your processes and reducing time wasted managing your business' expenses

- Make sure you are always getting the best value for your business and your clients

- Work with your team to streamline day to day processes and introduce savings seamlessly

Who is this book for?

1. Multi-site businesses such as restaurants, bars, caterers, care homes, doctor's surgeries and medical clinics

2. Established enterprises juggling multiple contracts, who want to reduce time they spend reviewing service options

3. Growing businesses that feel the pain of not having a procurement team in place

4. Young entrepreneurs that are considering introducing an expense management policy and do not know where to start

5. Businesses who are reviewing their expense management policy and want to achieve the best possible outcome

I've written *"How to survive and thrive in the time of living wage"* workbook to help you find pennies in unexpected nooks and crannies of your business operations, with a view of improving budgets for other aspects of your activities or even free funds to invest in new opportunities.

Nicholas Challen

Chapter 1
FOOD

- Planning,
- Procurement
- Storage

Why is this a problem?

Food prices chop and change every day. Suppliers do try to maximise their margins – and so should you. Do you have the time to thoroughly go through every single invoice every day? Did you know that with some useful strategies in place you can achieve up to 15% savings in the area of procurement alone? Think about what that would mean for your business – extra 15% profit or investment.

We look at three aspects that can generate most savings for businesses that are handling food:
- Planning
- Procurement
- Storage

Restaurants and hotels that spend more than £10,000 on food and drink per week are going to benefit most from the ideas discussed in this chapter. If your organisation spends less in the area, it is still reviewing the strategies, however be aware that the savings may be proportionally less and thinking about any changes, consider return on investment. After all, it's about saving your business the money and limiting expenses in the long term.

Why are we looking for savings in this area?

In hotels and restaurants food is – and is always going to be – a significant area of cost. As such, it should always be the first area we analyse in order to highlight potential areas with room for improvement. I look at procurement and storage as these areas are stages most businesses that have anything to do with food, have to deal with. It gives me a chance to give you advice most of will be able to implement in their organisations.

Also, in my experience in working with restaurants and catering businesses, I have noticed that these are the areas the saying we are creatures of habit is very highly visible. What I mean by that is these are the areas we tend not to review and renew our systems often enough. This may be following another saying „do not fix what isn't broken". However, if we are not reviewing and not checking, how can we be sure that it's not really doing any damage? How can we be sure that it can't be doing better? We have to be honest with ourselves and accept that assumptions and traditions in these three situations: planning, procurement and storage, may not always work to our advantage. We need to make sure they do.

Solution

So, how to find those unexpected savings? Let's take a closer look.

PLANNING

Say you are opening a new brand of a restaurant. You are going all out and you plan to open three locations at the same time. How to make sure you are getting the best deal on food? It's an item that moves in price rapidly, day to day.

An experienced chef will know by season what's the average he should be paying. Bear in mind that your chef is going to have at least one delivery of fresh produce per day and they are not going to have the time to sit and double check that the invoices are all correct against the prices they may have been quoted. Typically, a food supplier may provide a weekly pricelist or a price guide and just checking whether daily prices correspond with the weekly quote creates a considerable amount of admin.

Something that easily goes unnoticed, what should truly be considered is that it is common practice for suppliers to provide a cheap pricelist to secure the business and then gradually increase prices over the period of six months. If this goes unnoticed, half a year down the road you will not be getting the great deal you may think you are. That is definitely something to look out for. You could be changing your suppliers every three months with a view of securing those initial good deals perpetually, however consider the amount of hassle.

The colour of money

You want colour to lift a plate, but if you are using raspberries to liven up the dessert, remember the obvious – strawberries out of season can have a very jolly price. What other "raspberries" do you have in your menu? How can it be improved, without compromising the client experience?

Again, focus on ROI – do you have the people in your team that can dedicate their time to this task? Can you design a menu and outsource procurement?

PROCUREMENT

I write to you from a position of poacher-turned-gamekeeper within the food industry. I supplied hotels and restaurants in the South East for 25 years and hence I learned how suppliers make their margins and where savings can be made. Some of it comes down to buying power and the numbers game margins vs volume. If you are an aspiring restauranteur and/or you are in the early stages of creating a chain or network of eating places, you may not be in the position to negotiate those savings yet. Still, you may be able to find a partner that does: a procurement specialist, a strategic partner in a form of another food-business... The trick is to find your way into increasing your buying – negotiating – power.

How to do it:

- **Collect all food invoices from the last 6 months**
- **Search for patterns**

Only two steps, but it does take time. 6 months is enough to show what works and what does not. It's a time long enough to highlight any alarm bells. It may take a few weeks to do it, but it is worth it.

My experience shows that this analysis, combined with the appropriate buying power, can give you 15% saving in this area alone. What does 15% saving mean for you? Where would you like to invest that money?

STORAGE

According to currently available data* food sector produces 600,000 tonnes of food waste every year. 400,000 tonnes of which could have been avoided.

How much of food is your business throwing away? It may be hard to remember what the figure is per annum, so just consider how much food have you thrown away las week? Now multiply that by 52 and you will have an approximate figure. According to statistics, 2/3 could have been saved. How much would that mean to you in monetary terms? Would that saving help your budget?

This section will prove to you that it can be done. I will give you some useful and actionable tips on how to make it happen and start saving those pennies and pounds for your business today. Questions I am going to list here are so obvious, we often forget about them:

- **FIFO rule rules**

FIFO (First In, First Out) rule can help you save money and improve day to day operations, so apply it to cold and dry storage.

- **Keep it tight**

Air-tight containers will help you make sure food stored safely and increase its shelf life.

- **Keep cool**

Are you storing them at the right temperature? Are you controlling the humidity? Every refrigeration appliance should be equipped with a thermometer allowing you to check food is stored at the optimum temperature and that the unit performs as it should, without wasting power.

Hot topic: temperature

If you don't have them yet, look into the possibility of installing refrigeration units that measure the temperature of the items in the room, rather than air.

These are less power-hungry and will give you more accurate readings of the state of affairs.

- **Optimum capacity**

Avoid overloading your fridges as this can lead to a malfunction and spoiling all the food. Also, be sure to keep the air vents unobstructed, otherwise the conditions may become unsafe.

Case study

Type of business: Restaurant
Size: 160 covers
Expenses: £500,000 spent on food annually

We analysed all key items of food – including meat, fish – reviewed six months' worth of invoicing to detect any patterns and room for improvement, and looked at what point in the food chain is the food being thrown away. What transpired is that the items that is left on the plates and returns to the kitchens most often is garnish. This particular restaurant uses 40 punnets of corn salad a week.

Very few people eat garnish, so when it comes back to the kitchen, it's thrown away. The savings achieved on this item was £1 per punnet per week. This adds up to £40 per week. Over the course of the year, that's £2080 saving** – on garnish!

When have *you* thought about the savings you could make on garnish? Also, if it's possible to save that much on salad, what else is possible?

* http://www.wrap.org.uk/content/food-waste-hospitality-and-food-service-sector-0

 **In this case we were able to generate £32,000 savings per annum and we achieved it b reviewing not only food, but energy suppliers and merchant card services suppliers.

Analyse this

- Check operating margins

- Review suppliers (both prices and quality)

- Review constantly

In my experience, if you do all this, savings of 15% is what you could expect to achieve. What would a 15% increase to your budget mean to you?

NOTES

....
....
....
....
....
....
....
....
....
....
....
....
....

Areas to review today:

How often do you hear "this is how we've always done things" in your business, when it comes to planning, procurement and storage? Is this reason enough to continue in the same manner? I am not inviting you to start revolutions in your business' for the sake of the change, but I am wholeheartedly encouraging you to review them and make sure what works and what does not. When you KNOW that, you can make educated decisions that will benefit your business and help you improve your bottom line.

Are new deliveries put at the back on the shelves in order to make products with the shortest "use by" dates more visible and easily accessible?
It's common sense and a common practice in high street supermarket chains. Not all of their strategies are worthy of adapting to our business, but this one certainly is. Items to look out for: milk and dairy. If you are ordering a lot of milk and it's not stored properly, it can cost you dearly.

At what point in the food chain is the food being thrown away? How much food ends up in the bin? Why does it end up in the bin? Is it going bad, because we are not using enough of it? Is it going bad because the storage facility is not as efficient as it used to? Is it going bad at all? Are the portions too big? Perhaps customers' preferences have changed? What does not get eaten? Take notice of what comes back uneaten. Do your waiting staff ask customers if they enjoyed the food? You may need to make changes to the menu. Observe. Adapt and save money. Fail to react and, well, that's it – nothing will change, nothing will improve.

Do you plan ahead or simply go ahead?
It can really make a difference. It can save you pounds on strategic produce, ensure timely delivery and ensure quality of foods you are after.

NOTES

....
....
....
....
....
....
....
....
....
....
....
....
....
....
....
....
....
....
....
....
....
....

Chapter 2
ENERGY

- What to look out for before entering a contract
- What to do when a bill is too high
- How to minimise spend

Why is this a problem?

We can manage our energy in two ways:

- **By spending less on what you use**
- **By using less**

There is one fact that all business owners and managers responsible for procurement need to realise: prices of energy are not regulated. Does this mean that our businesses are at their mercy?

Not exactly.

It means, however, that it is us to us to realise the rules of the game and stand up for ourselves. What I mean by that is that we cannot be afraid to ask the questions.

The trick is to ask the right ones.

Why are we looking for savings in this area?

Lucky numbers:
6, 9, 13

You should be paying no more than 13p per unit day rates and 6-9 p night? Check how much you are paying. It all depends on circumstances, but if you are paying more, then the matter is worth investigating. (Energy prices at time of going to press July 2016)

Running a business is an absorbing task and bills can be difficult to understand, so we hardly ever spend time reading them, let alone question their accuracy. Even less of us will take time to check whether we have the correct type of energy meter installed. We assume that the service provider has done their best and that the amount on the bill is what we should pay. In some cases it is not and it is worth checking it.

Solution

PLANNING MANAGE YOUR ENERGY BY SPENDING LESS ON WHAT YOU USE

Figuring out how to spend less on what you use inevitably means examining bills. Admittedly, this is not the most pleasurable of reads, as it often looks like trying to read a coded letter.

Break the code

Understanding your bill is crucial to uncovering areas in which savings can be made. From making sure you are on the best tariff to choosing whether a contract is the best option for your business. The other source of making sure you have the optimum energy solution for your business is analysing its lifecycle. Although time consuming, it is worth it. If you have a procurement department, they should be doing this on a regular basis, to make sure you are getting the best deal. If you are a manager whose many responsibilities include taking care of this side of business, I've included a list of few helpful questions at the end of this chapter.

These documents are usually full of specific terms and energy providers seem to revel in coming up with new tariff names, which adds to the confusion. If you can spend time on it though, it is worth reading your energy bill documents thoroughly, as you may see it in a whole new light.

Here's a guide that may help you get to the information highlighting areas where savings could be made. Let me break down how a typical energy bill looks like and where the most popular pitfalls lie:

Your unique account/ customer number

Your unique contract number

Date when your payments is due

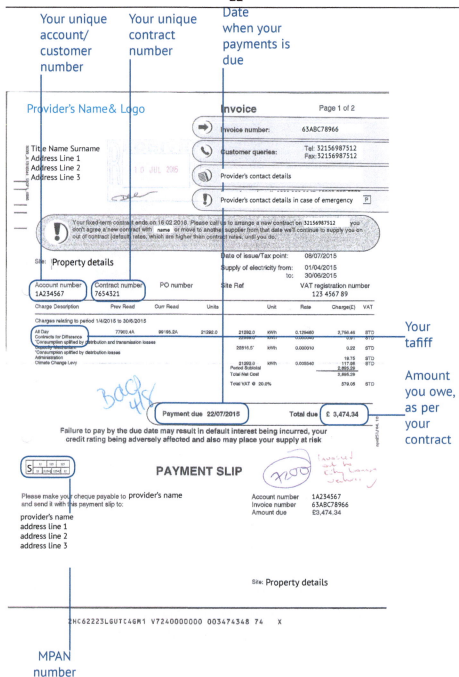

Provider's Name& Logo

Invoice   Page 1 of 2

Invoice number: 63ABC78966

Customer queries: Tel: 32156987512
Fax: 32156987512

Provider's contact details

Provider's contact details in case of emergency

Title Name Surname
Address Line 1
Address Line 2
Address Line 3

1 0 JUL 2015

Your fixed-term contract ends on 16 02 2016. Please call us to arrange a new contract on 32156987512   you
don't agree a new contract with   name   or move to another supplier from that date we'll continue to supply you on
out of contract (default) rates, which are higher than contract rates, until you do.

Site: Property details

Date of issue/Tax point: 08/07/2015
Supply of electricity from: 01/04/2015
to: 30/06/2015

Account number   Contract number   PO number   Site Ref   VAT registration number
1A234567   7654321   123 456 89

Charge Description	Prev Read	Curr Read	Units		Unit	Rate	Charge(£)	VAT
Charges relating to period 1/4/2015 to 30/6/2015								
All Day	77903.4A	99195.2A	21292.0	21292.0	kWh	0.129460	2,756.46	STD
Contracts for Difference				22399.0	kWh	0.000040	0.91	STD
*Consumption uplifted by distribution and transmission losses								
Capacity Mechanism				22816.5*	kWh	0.000010	0.22	STD
*Consumption uplifted by distribution losses								
Administration							19.75	STD
Climate Change Levy				21292.0	kWh	0.005540	117.95	STD
					Period Subtotal		2,895.29	
					Total Net Cost		2,895.29	
					Total VAT @ 20.0%		579.05	STD

Your tafiff

Amount you owe, as per your contract

Payment due 22/07/2015   Total due   £ 3,474.34

Failure to pay by the due date may result in default interest being incurred, your
credit rating being adversely affected and also may place your supply at risk

S | 12 | 123 | 123
   | 12 | 1234 | 1234 | 12

PAYMENT SLIP

Invoiced
ot to
Cuty Lamse
Jahun

Please make your cheque payable to **provider's name**
and send it with this payment slip to:

provider's name
address line 1
address line 2
address line 3

Account number   1A234567
Invoice number   63ABC78966
Amount due   £3,474.34

Site: Property details

2HC62223LGUTC4GM1 V7240000000 003474348 74   X

MPAN number

MPAN NUMBER

One information often missing on the bill is when the contract expires. To find that out, you need to contact your provider, instruct your broker to do so and a broker needs to go through a bill verification process. There are three main types of rates:

- **Contract**

A fixed price agreement over an agreed period; as energy prices are in constant state of flux, too long a contracts may not be as beneficial as we usually believe; it is best to consult an energy broker who can analyse not only the price of energy per unit, but consider energy consumption and character of a business as well and then suggest the optimum solution

- **Out of contract**

Always more expensive than a fixed term contract prices, out of contract prices usually apply to users who wish to switch providers over a period when an existing contract expired and a new contract hasn't started yet

- **Deemed rates**

Following the British law, energy supply is not assigned to the property owner, but to the property, so when someone new takes over a property, they are deemed to have entered into an contract and are deemed to pay existing rates until a new contract supersedes the existing arrangement

Each meter has a number assigned to this particular property, it's called a meter Point Administration Number (MPAN), Supply Number or an S Number. Each has 21 digits and can be found on your energy bill, displayed in this format:

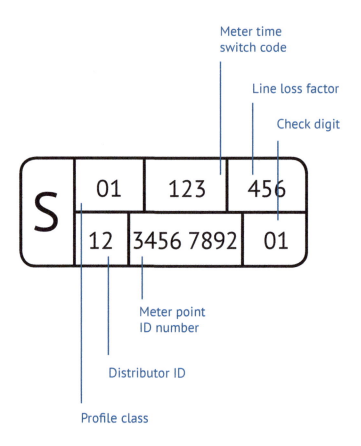

Each MPAN characterises corresponds with a tariff, which summarises how the energy provider believes you are going to be using the energy on a daily basis.

WHICH METER IS BEST FOR MY BUSINESS?

First two numbers in this sequence refer to a Profile Class.

* Households are assigned numbers beginning with 01 and 02

Also, all care homes should check whether they are assigned a 01 or 02 meter; although they are a business, due to its characteristics the energy is used as in a home, so here 5% VAT applies. I recently came across a group of care homes where the amount of unclaimed VAT reached £300,000 – it's a serious oversight that in many cases can be the difference between scraping by and turning a serious profit.

Businesses are assigned numbers between 03 and 08, where:

* 00 – large consumption, HH (half hourly meter), these have KVA rating (KVA stands for 1,000 volt amps) to ensure the power you need to use is made available.
* 03 means Non-Domestic Unrestricted,
* 04 Non-Domestic Economy 7
* 05 Non-Domestic Maximum Demand 0-20% Load Factor
* 06 Non-Domestic Maximum Demand 20-30% Load Factor
* 07 Non-Domestic Maximum Demand 30-40% Load Factor
* 08 Non-Domestic Maximum Demand >40% Load Factor

MANAGING YOUR ENERGY BY USING LESS

Take action

I always begin with ways of decreasing energy consumption that require little or no investment at all. This means you can start implementing them instantly. Again, this is a strategy of making many little changes that can make a big impact when combined.

> # "Stand by" mode
> # costs money too
>
> A computer screen being left on stand-by can use up to £40 worth of energy per year. How many computers are there in your office?

Education and engagement

Consider telling your employees how much you are spending on energy. Saying "we are spending too much" or using expressions like "energy is way too expensive these days" are often too abstract to make a lasting impression. If you disclose an actual figure, the situations becomes real and then something can be done about it.

Why not go a step further and engage your employees in the efforts to spend less on energy? One of my clients implemented this scenario and said they were spending £20,000 on energy per annum. They were looking to reduce it to £15,000. He also said that if the target is reached by the end of the year, he will divide £5,000 and share half of it with the team as an end-of-year bonus. What a great way to promote employee engagement and take effective action.

Payback

Now it's time to look at payback – if we are going to invest anything, what is going to yield the biggest return. For example:

- **Buildings**
o   Are windows being left open?
o   Are computers being left on overnight
o   Are toilets light being left on? Sensors are a relatively low cost option of alleviating human error, so this is definitely one thing worth considering
o   Consider unused or rarely used spaces like storerooms - sensors controlling the light could contribute to noticeable savings every year
o   LED lighting is 80% more efficient than conventional lighting; would switching be an option in your business?
o   Insulation – there are many local schemes helping fund building insulation, it is wort making that call to your local council

- **Operational changes**
o   Voltage optimisation

for most electrical equipment in the UK is designed to work at 240V, but most of our electrical equipment works to an European standard of 225V and the difference just goes to waste, the excess just gets lost in the grid; there is equipment you can purchase that will adjust the amount of power; it's a proposition for heavy energy users, so if you are paying in excess of £100k for energy per annum, it's worth investigating

o   Air conditioning

keep it serviced and clean for optimised performance and reduced energy loss

o   Heating

Check how old your boiler is and consider changing, if it's more than 15 years old; you can even look at significant savings if it's it's possible to lower the temperature setting by 1^0

o   Refrigerating

please refer to the previous chapter (page 16) for details

- **Renewables**

Going green is a great way of saving energy, however the initial investment is significant and from that point of view this solution is not viable for every business. It is definitely worth considering by companies with high energy consumption, like hotels, spa centres with pools and saunas. Especially if they have reasonable space for solar panels or would consider ground water heating as part of their green policy.

Residential care homes need to make sure they are on a right meter (01 or 02) and VAT rating – here, a residential rate applies, so it should be 5%, not 20%!

The optimal environment

The longer we sit in an office, the colder the temperature seems to be, just because we are not generating enough body heat. It may be worth introducing hourly exercise breaks for the team to increase productivity and manage heating cost.

Optimum workplace temperature guidelines can be found on the Health and Safety Executive website http://www.hse.gov.uk/temperature/faq.htm

NOTES

....
....
....
....
....
....
....
....
....
....

ESOS

Have you heard about Energy Saving Opportunity Scheme (ESOS)? It's relevant, for large companies, which ESOS regulations define as any UK company that either:

• "employs 250 or more people, or

• has an annual turnover in excess of 50 million euro (£38,937,777), and an annual balance sheet total in excess of 43 million euro (£33,486,489)

• an overseas company with a UK registered establishment which has 250 or more UK employees (paying income tax in the UK)"

If you believe your business is going to reach this level in the next 4 years, you need to supply your application. Full guidelines can be found here https://www.gov.uk/guidance/energy-savings-opportunity-scheme-esos, however it comes down to having a proper energy policy. If you have multiple sites, each needs to have such a document and undergo an assessment. It may be worth checking with your energy broker to see if they would act as your lead assessor and prepare the application for you.

Case study

Type of business: Local supermarket
Expenses: £55,000 reduced by almost £24,000

Before they contacted me, they hadn't had a bill for a year and when it finally arrived, the total was just over £55,000. The bill revealed that they were paying out of contract rates at 22.4 pence per unit, which is ridiculously expensive. The bill suggested they were on a fixed rate contract as the phrase "Your fixed energy plan end on the (the date was given)". This was misleading as they they've actually gone for out of contract rates.

At this point alarm bells rang an I was contacted. We contacted the provider to confirm what our contractual status was. In the end, we were able to negotiate a price 11p per unit.

What's even better, the whole bill had been reviewed to reflect this new price, which should have been applied in the first place. Result – a year's worth of energy and a saving of almost £24,000.

This can be an employee's salary or an investment in new equipment.

Areas to review today:

Be very careful when you are discussing contracts

Verbal agreement constitutes a beginning of a new contract. Take our case study, for example. The initial cost per unit was 22.4p. Say the provider wants to keep a client and offers to drop the price to 15p per unit, if you enter a 2 year contract. The natural reaction is to say, 7.4p saving is a great result. If you say "15p for two years, that seems fine, I'll go with that" – at that point it's legally binding from that moment. 15p is a reasonable improvement over 24.4p, yes – but that is not the best price they can offer. If we were to say yes to that offer over the phone, that would be the end of the negotiation. We would still have to pay 30% more than the 11p per unit we were able to achieve in the end.

Check if you are paying a competitive price

The bill will tell you how much you are paying per unit. If it is more than 13p per unit, you may want to investigate why you are paying so much and what may be changed.

Check whether you are in a contract or not

Some suppliers will tell you that on your bill, some not. Even if your bill states that your current energy plan is going to end at a certain date, that does not mean you have a contract with them! It sounds like it, but this may as well mean that you are paying out of contract rates. Unfortunately, you need to call your provider and ask them directly.

Ask yourself how much is your time worth?

There are over 20 energy providers out there, each with various tariffs. Is it practical to dedicate your, or your employees time, to check them all and find the best deal? Using an energy broker is the most effective way, as it is their job to monitor available energy tariffs. They will also consider the way you use the energy and suggest an optimum solution for your business. What's more, they usually earn their money on the savings made, so it is in their interest to negotiate the best deal. It is a good solution for businesses of all sizes.

NOTES

Chapter 3
MERCHANT CARD SERVICES

- What to look out for
- How can it affect the bottom line and customer experience

Why is this a problem?

There are two main issues with merchant card services: technology and cost.

Technology

When it comes to technology, most of the UK suppliers are using third party suppliers to equip their clients with Electronic Point of Sale (EPOS) systems, till systems, etc. Unfortunately, this leads to severe delays in solving any issues. Having to wait 4-6 weeks, which have become a norm, for a new terminal is a lifetime in retail and when it happens in a busy season, this can be a death sentence for a small or medium-sized business.

In addition, thirst party suppliers tend to use refurbished machines. This carries significant risks of malfunction, not only due to increased probability of malfunctioning, which causes delays in daily operations of a machine in question, but also compatibility with new systems.

We've gained a client due to that very reason. Just before Christmas a chain of retail shops using a certain brand of older machines, tried update the software. What was supposed to be a routine operation, knocked out all of the machines. We are not talking about one location. This affected every store, throughout UK – just before Christmas, the busiest retail time of the year.

Cost

I am guessing you are familiar with the PPI scandal, where financial products where mis-sold to businesses and individuals throughout the UK. Regrettably, a similar thing has happened in the world of merchant card services. Any business that takes card payments needs to be PCI DSS (Payment Card Industry Data Security Standards) compliant. It comes down to updating your application once a year, online, to make sure you are compliant with current data protection laws and best practice incentives.

High street banks will manage PCI compliancy for the clients. 70% of the market have their cards with their bank and they offer to manage the PCI compliancy for them, which is fine if they do. However, some do not. The reason being is if they leave their clients not compliant, they can charge them an added percentage per each transaction. This adds up to much bigger costs for you, the business owner. We do all we can to improve the customer experience and when they buy into our philosophy and finally want to purchase our product or service, we want to make it as easy and swift as possible. Unfortunately, when merchant card services are involved, this sometimes backfires.

It is especially noticeable in restaurants in the busy evening hours, when people queue to get in, but are blocked by people who cannot get out. They have finished their meal and the experience was magical, sadly all that hard work was spoilt, by them having to wait long minutes by the terminal. Or even having to organise cash payment if the terminal goes rogue altogether. In this line of business, time is money and I mean this literally. Minutes wasted at the terminal are minutes your team are not using to service more clients and this means lost money. In addition, this can put a dent on the image of the brand and instead of streamlining the service, create an unnecessary barrier to profit.

Why are we looking for savings in this area?

Unfortunately, there is no such thing as an average fee per merchant card transaction. There are too many factors to take into account and an average number would be too removed from the truth. When figuring out the best rate though we need to consider type of business (for instance bridal shops, as they take deposits so far in advance actual service, are deemed 'high risk' and have to deal with high merchant card fees), how the business operates (does it take more credit or debit card payments), to start with. The data can help us negotiate the best deal. For example, if you are taking more credit card payments, we could negotiate a deal with higher debit card payment rates and this would not affect your day to day, but could help us bring the cost of credit card transactions down. This puts a pressure on some businesses and forces them to apply a minimum charge limit, which clients are not fond of. If you knew that you are get-ting the best deal available, this would alleviate the need for that sort of house rule and increase the customer satisfaction. Merchant card services are supposed to make the payment making process simpler and by choosing the right provider we can save both time and money.

Solution

Make sure you're merchant card supplier is a one-stop shop for all your needs. This will make the service smoother and bring your costs down, by reducing losses. Analyse your merchant statement and look at the extra charges you may be incurring. If you have never heard about PCI compliancy before, chances are your provider has promised to take care of it for you. Make sure that they do! If not, you may be charged more than you have to for the privilege of using a card terminal in your business.

Ask your provider to explain what PCI compliancy is and how to do it. If they are willing to do it for you, but it costs more than a fiver to do so, you are paying too much.

Case studies

1.   A client of ours broke a terminal, it was accidentally dropped on the stairs. They phoned their consultant directly. He then contacted the head office, with an in-house technical team, who picked a machine from the shelf, programmed it and sent it off the same day. Problem solved.

2.   Hair salon owner set up a business bank account and needed a PDQ machine as well. She waited, called, set up a date with a bank but no one came. She came to us and within 10 days the paperwork was

processed, terminal programmed and her personal consultant was back in her salon showing her how to use the machine.

3.   Recently I have helped a client save money on insurance and food (£32000 annual saving!), however they entered a 5-year merchant card services contract prior to me meeting them. Had they waited, we could have saved them £1500 per annum. And £600 on telecoms.

Areas to review today:

If you feel like you're only option to break even is to charge your customers a 50p fee per card transaction, contact a broker to see if they can negotiate a better deal for you. Merchant card services should be an advantage for your business, not a burden!

The queue is growing, and the terminal is disconnecting If a terminal is disconnecting during rush hours... it's an alarm bell that may be a sign that your terminal is a refurbished one just with a new keypad put on it. Investigate!

If you are still waiting for your provider to set up a system for you... If you are setting up a merchant card payment system at a new location and sorting it out takes weeks instead of days – shop around, because you are not getting the best service. Customer service delays prior to installation are, unfortunately, a good indication of a customer service you may receive later on.

Who actually provides you with a system

Is it the company you are engaging to do that or a thirst party? Major high street banks are usually using a third party suppliers, so it's worth double checking who you are actually working with. Dealing with a third party carries significant risks of delays, should anything go wrong with the system. It is quite common to wait 4-6 weeks for a new machine. Can your business wait that long? If not, make sure you're supplier keeps everything in house.

Shop around When setting up a business account we are asked if we need a payment system. It seems easy to tick a box and go with your high street bank. However, that may not be the best option for your business. Shop around, ask a broker – it's a good investment.

NOTES

....
....
....
....
....
....
....
....
....
....
....

Chapter 4
TELECOMS, IT & DATA DISPOSAL

- What we do not know, can still affect the business
- Highlighting the risks
- Tips on how to get it right

Why is this a problem?

We can hardly spend more than a few moments without a wi-fi, even during a meeting at a local coffee shop.

Now, imagine your life without a phone.

Just for one day.

Would you feel like you are missing out? Your business definitely would.

Reliability, speed and security are the three pillars of an effective service – and all three are we expect to be provided to us. You probably know that if you are collecting your clients' data you are also responsible for its security. Did you know, however, that also means you are responsible for that data's safe disposal? In this chapter, we focus on the savings connected to making sure we run operations smoothly, provide data security for our operations and so avoid fines.

Better safe than sorry!

GETTING THE DATA IS ONE THING, STORING AND DISPOSING OF THEM - ANOTHER

When security of data storage is an area that gets more and more recognition, mostly due to well-publicised security breaches of prominent organisations. What I want to emphasize, it does apply to businesses of all sizes. When it comes to data protection, you cannot be too careful.

You need to encrypt all sensitive data, even if you carry it on a pendrive
In 2013 a memory stick with sensitive information got lost and the employer, North East Lincolnshire Council, got served with a penalty of £80,000. The Information Commissioner's Office is on the lookout for any data breaches, so knowing what you need to do can save you a lot of money. The best source of information will be an organisation that specialises in data security or your broker, who works with a tried and tested one.

Pressing 'delete' on your keyboard is not enough to wipe the data out from your PC
Every now and again we upgrade the equipment in our businesses, what do you do with the old computers? Deleting everything from your old hard drive before you dispose of an old PC is no longer sufficient. Unfortunately, data disposal is an area so often ignored by businesses and can cost them dearly. Beware.

How to make sure your computer's memory is professionally wiped out?
The answer is in the question – get a professional in to erase the memory

It can become personal

Since 2010, the Data Protection Act was reviewed to include serious penalties:

- Fines of up to £500,000 for serious contraventions of the DPA

- Prison Sentences for deliberate or negligent customer data leaks by individuals within an organisation.

In addition, to promote proper data disposal, Monetary Penalty Notices and the ICO's Code currently place direct **PERSONAL** responsibility on many company directors and managers.

of your old computers and mobile devices, BEFORE you get rid of them. As long as a shadow of data remains on those hard drives, you are responsible for its safety.

Why are we looking for savings in this area?

With telecoms, it's easy to get yourself stuck in a 5-year contract with a provider that does not offer the best deal.

Sometimes businesses get tempted by low rates, only to find out they were looking at prices for private users. Like with energy, there's an array of providers and even more services and tariffs out there. It takes time to understand them, even before we start comparing. The trick is to understand how a certain service can work within your business.

Solution

You need to analyse how you are going to use your telecoms and IT:

- Are you going to make or take more calls?

- Do you need a business line for the premises

- Will your employees need mobiles as well?

- Are you going to retain sensitive data of your clients?

- How are you planning to dispose of the data?

Analyse all this with the future of your business in mind. There is no other choice but to compare and contrast, shop around.

Of course, a good broker can take this hassle away from you and do the comparing for you. However, even a broker will want to know the answers to the above questions. They will need to understand what type of business you are and what are your plans – in other words, what are your habits as a user?

Areas to review today:

NOTES

If you collect data about your clients, how do you store it?

Are any of your employees carrying the data on portable devices? If you are planning an upgrade, how are you going to dispose of the data stored on all the devices?

Make sure the service you are getting is suitable to the way you work

Analyse the way you operate as a business and use this information to find the best service – or show it to your broker to help him understand your needs and devise the best solution.

Can your provider grow with you?

Consider not only what you need now but how do you see your business developing within the next 5-10 years. Is your provider able to scale the operations up as you grow?

Back-up plan

Things can go wrong even with the state of the art equipment, so ask about what happens in case of a systems failure. What's their emergency policy?

How quickly will they be able to get you back online? Are there any additional costs to be considered?

Installation, training, support

Find out how they plan to install new systems and are they going to train you. Ask about when it's supposed to happen and how long is it going to take? Are you going to have to shut the operations down for one day? Can they work around your schedule? If you have any questions – can you contact them direct? What's the response time?

Do they want to give you the answers

Ask, ask and then ask some more. Test their knowledge and experience. Are they giving you comprehensive answers?

NOTES

....
....
....
....
....
....
....
....
....
....
....
....
....
....
....
....

Chapter 5
WASHROOMS
& WASTE DISPOSAL

- Risks and opportunities
- Contract management
- Best practices

Why is this a problem?

This chapter is dedicated to restaurant and hotel owners, however it is relevant to all who employ female staff and/or have female visitors to their premises. In this day and age it is hard to come up with a business that does not qualify under one of the two criterions.

This is not going to be a chapter about how important cleanliness is, as I would hope that would be stating the obvious, but rather about ways of managing it efficiently. This is often a problem that may result in falling standards or in breaching the legislation, albeit unwillingly.

Since 1992[1] all companies are required by law to arrange for the appropriate disposal of sanitary dressings in ladies washrooms. In addition, Environmental Protection Act 1990[2] places a duty of care on

1. http://www.legislation.gov.uk/uksi/1992/3004/contents/made
2. http://www.legislation.gov.uk/ukpga/1990/43/contents

you, the business; this means you are responsible for the correct disposal of any waste that comes from your premises. It is your duty to make sure this waste is dealt with properly, not only while it remains at your premises, but after it leaves it too and until it's finally disposed of. Failing to do so may result in considerable fines.[1]

Why are we looking for savings in this area?

Abiding by the legislation and avoiding fines is one way of reducing outgoings in business. But I believe we have an opportunity of improving operations in an area of business activity that is often overlooked or deemed insignificant.

Yet, every little saving can add up to a substantial sum by the time we are doing our accounts. Even small contracts can be negotiated and, especially in larger organisations, there is an opportunity of improving quality of services (and saving some money) when we consider an option of consolidating services we are outsourcing.

Reviewing 5 contracts annually is surely a better option than having to review and renew 15 agreements. It is not always possible, or viable to do so, but it is worth spending some time to consider whether that is an option in your business. You can save yourself a significant amount of time and money.

1. Environment Agency, Annual report and accounts for the year 2014 to 2015

https://www.gov.uk/government/uploads/system/uploads/attachment_data/file/442886/LIT_10133.pdf

Want not, waste not

I talk extensively about food waste management and disposal in the first chapter, so if you're managing a food related business, go to page 9 to revisit best practices in this area.

Solution

So, when the number of contracts you have with your suppliers overwhelms you, it is time to consider nominating a member of staff to a position of your procurement specialist or contact a broker and get an expert to act on your behalf.

- **create a calendar of contract renewals** Having all your contract renewal dates written down will help you act with plenty of time to spare. This way you will have enough time to ask all the right questions, consider alternative solutions and various providers.

- **create a list of your priorities** Various service providers have different contracts and it may be difficult comparing their offers. If you define a list of what is important for your business and when you want it to happen, you will know that the price you are getting covers the services that are essential to your business.

- **do not be afraid to negotiate** What's the worst that can happen? The quote will not change, but if you ask, you may get a bigger value for money.

Savings
by design

Is your washroom designed to save energy and water?

There is more than one way to flush a toilet, wash your hands and dry them:

- efficient air hand dryers can save you up to 80% of energy, compared with the older models

- push taps or appliances with motion sensors can significantly reduce our water consumption

- motion sensor light can also help you save energy, especially if it's LED

Case study

Type of business: Residential centre for people with learning difficulties
Size: 22 locations
Result: 40 contracts reduced to 1

In early 2015 I was put in touch with a client, who managed all their suppliers and contracts in house. This was, among other duties, a responsibility of their office staff. This is not uncommon, for business with no procurement department, to assign this duty to their existing staff. However, over the years the number of contracts and suppliers grew and when I was contacted it exceeded forty.

Imagine having to deal with renewals of forty contracts each year! Reviewing existing options, often putting it to tender, managing candidates, etc...

Where this is just one of the duties you need to take care of, it becomes necessary to renew the contract, simply because you cannot dedicate necessary time to shop around for alternative options – not when you have to review a contract and a supplier every week.

This particular organisation's resources were overstretched and that is why they contacted me to help. I acted as their external procurement department and approached the situation with a view of saving time and money.

The first was achieved by carefully reviewing existing contract and analysing any possibilities of consolidating services provided by various suppliers. Less suppliers mean improved service and, usually, more amicable rates, which leads us to negotiating better contracts. In this case we were able to save them 15% per annum and reduce 40 contracts to 1.

Areas to review today:

Make sure your suppliers are aware of the latest acts and regulations and are compliant. Make sure that the service provider dealing with waste from your premises supplies you with 'duty of care' certificates and keeps your documentation up to date in order to make sure you comply with all necessary regulations as well.

Can your supplier grow with your business? Choose the one that can. It will save you changing the provider in the future and may help you negotiate better rates, as a long standing existing client.

Create a list of your priorities – can these services be provided by one supplier? Wherever possible, reduce the amount of contracts you have to deal with. This will free a substantial amount of time in your business, will give you a chance to review the remaining suppliers thoroughly and compare and contract with alternative providers to choose the best option for your business. This should also make it easier to choose the right supplier for your business as you will know that the services that are being quoted are the ones your business really needs.

Make sure they are fit for the job. Remember, according to the Environmental Protection Act 1990 it is you who are responsible for all the waste produced at your premises, from the point of its origin to the moment of its ultimate disposal. It is your duty, therefore, to ensure that whoever deals with it on your behalf, is performing their responsibilities in an appropriate manner. It is especially important when you are dealing with clinical waste, which includes sharp objects like needles, biohazardous waste and offensive waste.

NOTES

....
....
....
....
....
....
....
....
....
....
....
....
....
....

Chapter 6
INSURANCE

- Compulsory vs advisable
- How to talk to talk to your broker
- When to revise your insurance

Why is this a problem?

Insurance has a bad reputation. It is so often treated as a chore, something imposed on a business owner, as if they do not have enough on their plate anyway.

True, choosing the right insurance, even making sure you have the correct one, is not the most exciting activity on your to do list, still, it is an important one. You should know what you are buying.

Yet, due to this attitude most of us just want to sort it out as quickly as possible and with least possible hassle. This often results in getting an ill-fitted policy or failing to notice when it stops being relevant to our business, which often cost money when what we need most is reassurance and financial support.

Why are we looking for savings in this area?

In the insurance game, it is vital to make sure that we are getting what we are paying for. This means spending some time reading the small print or asking your broker a few well-designed questions. In this chapter I want to prove to you that having that conversation is really important and beneficial to your business venture.

Failing to do so may result in paying for policies that are not fit for purpose – and that means wasting money. It may not be much in the beginning, but it all adds up, and the pay-out in the end may be significant.

Solution

What's compulsory for some businesses may be optional for others, so here's a handy list you can check your insurances against – or you can use it during your next conversation with your broker.

COMPULSORY VS ADVISABLE
Employers' liability insurance
If you have employees, the – by law – you need to have employer's liability insurance.
It begins at £5 million limit of indemnity, but £10 million is considered standard. Remember to make the certificate visible (you will receive it from your insurance provider).

NOTE: The Health and Safety Executive can fine companies up to £2500 per day for not holding employers liability insurance. There are certain exemptions though, for example family businesses (but not limited companies) and businesses employing solely their owner, so talk to your broker to make sure you have the right cover.

Motor insurance
If you have a fleet or if you are starting a fleet with just the one car, the minimum you are obliged to get is a third party liability insurance. This covers personal injury (unlimited) or property damage to third parties (at least £1 million) caused by any of your employees driving the insured vehicle.

Third party insurance is a requirement, but having a comprehensive motor policy is good practice. How important the vehicle is to your business? How would you replace it? Talk these questions through with your broker when choosing the best insurance solution.
Not compulsory, but strongly advised.

NOT COMPULSORY, BUT STRONGLY ADVISED
Public liability and product liability insurance
Whilst it is not required by law to have public and products liability, it is strongly advised, especially if you are producing, selling and repairing goods. Public liability would cover you should someone slip on an unmarked area of wet floor on your premises. Products liability would cover damage or injury as a direct result of your products. Importantly for food businesses, public and products liability would cover you against allegations that you have caused injury to the public, including food poisoning.

Property insurance We often think about our business as our home away from home and we should treat as such. Property insurance covers the contents of the restaurant, bar, hotel, the office and may also cover portable equipment.

Business interruption insurance

This one is especially worth looking into. It covers the loss of income, should your business be unable to operate as a result of a damage and can also cover additional expenditure during that time. Making sure you get this right can mean a difference between being reimbursed for the amount of income you would have lost in the event of a 2-week leak and just getting being repaid for the damaged stock. Food businesses are often heavily reliant on their location, be a high street or shopping centre, if the property is damaged or inaccessible, this will replace your income whilst your property is being restored.

Loss of income vs loss of gross profit

Loss of income must mirror the value of takings (gross revenue) over the course of a year. Loss of gross profit must mirror the value of profit you make in a year.

Businesses usually get one or the other. Make sure you know which one you have. There are businesses that are insured on a loss of income basis only thinking that it's their profit. Make sure you are not underinsured.

Loss of Licence Loss of licence is often and additional module that is available for food and restaurant businesses. Some insurers include loss of licence protection automatically, others charge a small additional premium. It covers reasonable costs and expenses for appeal against loss of licence. But remember, there is still onus on you as the licence holder to meet minimum requirements. There is no cover is you simply forget to renew your liquor licence.

Insurance, it's a good thing

Think about the insurance not as a necessary evil bit a tool that can ensure your business continuity.

Talk to your broker – a good one will welcome an opportunity to get to know your business – and make sure your insurance is up to date and periodically check for alternatives to make sure you are getting the best value for money.

Case study

How difficult would it be to replace all the furniture and accessories used to decorate your restaurant? There was a restauranteur that accumulated all the furniture over the course of a year. Most of it was second-hand and so his perception of the value was quite small. However, should he find himself in a position of having to replace it all at once, the cost of his chosen vintage décor would be significant. Luckily, we managed to insure him for the true value of the equipment with his business.

Areas to review today:

Have you outgrown your insurance?

If your business turnover reaches £500k per annum, you should have at least £500k worth of business interruption protection. Double check if the value of your insurance keeps up with the value/growth of your business. A good broker can often find appropriate cover without increasing the value of your monthly premiums, so it is worth having a chat with them.

Add renewal dates to your diary

Make a point of talking to your broker well in advance to give them a chance of getting you a better deal.

Have a conversation with your broker

A good broker will welcome an opportunity to have a chat with you. Make them go through the insurance with you, tell them what your business is all about and what are your plans for growth. Giving them more information allows them to give you the best value for money and choose a product that truly answers the needs of your business – that could add up in significant savings further down the line.

Value your wine

Count up the bottles and double check what is the actual value of your wine cellar. It may be worth more than you think. If you think that you have £5k in wines and spirits, but you actually have £10k, you are 50% underinsured, therefore some providers will only pay 50% worth of a claim.

YOUR WORKBOOK #1 FOOD
take action and start saving today:

AREAS TO REVIEW	OUTCOME	CONCLUSIONS & ACTIONS TO BE TAKEN (BY WHEN)
• Are new deliveries put at the back on the shelves?		
• Are all "use by" dates visible and accessible?		
• At what point in the food chain is the food being thrown away?		
• How much food ends up in the bin? Why?		
☐ too much ordered		
☐ not efficient storage		
☐ too big portions		
• Ordering sheets and invoices are checked regularly - how often?		
• Review your bills; check the last 6 months to identify the best price.		
• How much time does it take you or your staff?		

YOUR WORKBOOK #2 ENERGY
take action and start saving today:

AREAS TO REVIEW	OUTCOME	CONCLUSIONS & ACTIONS TO BE TAKEN (BY WHEN)
• Check if you are paying a competitive price - review 6 month of your energy bills. Are you getting the best price?		
• Check whether you are in a contract or not.		
• Check if you have the correct meter?		
• Review energy providers - is there anyone who can give you a better price?		
• Note how much time does this take you.		
• Note when is your next energy renewals and mark your calendar 8 weeks ahead of time to perform this check again.		

YOUR WORKBOOK #3
MERCHANT CARD SERVICES
take action and start saving today:

AREAS TO REVIEW	OUTCOME	CONCLUSIONS & ACTIONS TO BE TAKEN (BY WHEN)
• Do you process more credit or debit card payments? Can you get a better deal on one of them sacrificing the other?		
• Can you rely on your equipment? Does it freeze during busy hours? If so, how often?		
• Note who is your actual provider.		
• How's the customer service? Can you rely on their support?		
• Shop around: are you getting the best deal?		
• Note how much time does it take you to perform all these checks? Can you delegate?		

YOUR WORKBOOK #4
TELECOMS, IT & DATA DISPOSAL
take action and start saving today:

AREAS TO REVIEW	OUTCOME	CONCLUSIONS & ACTIONS TO BE TAKEN (BY WHEN)
• How do you store your client's data?		
• Do your employees carry your clients' data on portable devices?		
• Can your provider grow with your business' requirements?		
• What's your data back up plan?		
• What's your provider's emergency policy?		
• How quickly can they react?		
• Is there additonal cost?		
• Can you rely on their training & support?		

YOUR WORKBOOK #5
WASHROOMS & WASTE DISPOSAL
take action and start saving today:

AREAS TO REVIEW	OUTCOME	CONCLUSIONS & ACTIONS TO BE TAKEN (BY WHEN)
• Are your suppliers aware of the latest acts and regulations and are they compliant?		
• Do they provide you with necessary documentation?		
• Can your supplier grow with your business?		
• How many suppliers do you have to deal with?		
• Note when are the contracts due for renewal and mark your calendar 8 weeks ahead to give yourself time to shop around.		
• How much time does it take - can you delegate?		
• Are you getting the best deal?		

YOUR WORKBOOK #6
INSURANCE
take action and start saving today:

AREAS TO REVIEW	OUTCOME	CONCLUSIONS & ACTIONS TO BE TAKEN (BY WHEN)
• Check if your insurance is still appropriate to the size of your business.		
• Add renewal dates to your diary and make a note to shop around 8 weeks ahead of time.		
• Have a conversation with your broker - tell them about your business plans & goals.		
• Check if your inventory is insured to the appropriate value.		
• Do you have all the insurance you need?		
• Do you have any policies that you do not need at the moment?		
• How long does it take? Can you delegate?		

About the Author

Nicholas comes from a fresh produce back ground, both his father and grandfather working in the old Covent Garden Market in London. Father as a wholesaler and grandfather supplying fruit and vegetables to hotels, restaurants and clubs in the West End of London.

Nicholas continued the family tradition, and supplied fruit and vegetables to the catering trade, initially in Essex, then moved to the new Covent Garden Market, at one time supplying and finally moving to the Cotswolds running Poupart Evesham as the Branch Managing Director, supplying Country house hotels and Restaurants.

It all stems from one simple fact - I enjoy good food. Helping businesses spend less allows them to keep high standards, keep using excellent ingredients and keep dining an exquisite experience. I want to see more of that - in hotels, restaurants and bars - irrespective of the economic climate.

After 25 years of supplying food to hotels, when the business was sold Nicholas worked as an interim consultant, in particular to the hospitality sector, so has extensive experience supplying restaurants, but also working in restaurants. Recognising that he is not really suited to retail, Nicholas started

So I keep helping them find savings in unexpected places.

an energy consultancy business, advising on how to get energy as a better rate, this was very successful, but he yearned to be back dealing with the food industry – friends and colleagues notices that whenever Nicholas spoke about food he spoke with a passion, and it was clear this is where he belongs.

So in 2014, HBSL was born, a procurement consultancy, specifically designed to help hotels and restaurants review and reduce their costs whilst maintaining quality standards and service levels. This is at the core of everything HBSL does, and is now the company's mission statement.

HBSL – helping business spend less

Our mission – to save companies time and money whilst maintaining quality standards and service levels.

Visit our website for more tips www.hbsl-procurement.co.uk

NOTES

NOTES